US v Eric Adams: City of Maybe

Part I

by Matthew Russell Lee
Inner City Press

October - November, 2024

TABLE OF CONTENTS

Chapter 1: Eric Adams in the SDNY

Chapter 2: Electorate as Jury

Chapter 3: Eric Adams on the Silk Road

Chapter 4: Fire Department First

Chapter 5: Presentment before Magistrate Judge Parker

Chapter 6: Eric Adams in The Bronx

Chapter 7: October 2, 2024 Before Judge Ho

Chapter 8: FDNY Plea, Presentment of Bahi

Chapter 9: Circle (Firing Squad) of Commissioners

Chapter 10: Interlude, Bling Bishop Lamor Whitehead

Chapter 11: ICE Information, Straw Donors

Chapter 12: November 1, 2024 before Judge Ho

Chapter 13: Eric Adams and Election(s)

I. Eric Adams in the SDNY

It was May 24, 2022 in a garden next to the SDNY Federal courthouse. Eric Adams stood at the podium and ran thought his story, his campaign and elevator pitch: "Arrested at 15, negative encounters with the police… South Jamaica, Queens, going into the classroom and finding 'Dummy' written on the back of my chair… Never learned I had dyslexia until I was in college, tempted to drop out… But I turned pain into purpose."

The question, to some, was to what purpose?

Two and a half years later, Adams was back in SDNY, this time under Federal indictment for Turkish bribes and straw donors. He proclaimed his innocence and asked to move his trial up to April Fool's Day

2025, saying anything later would hurt his chances to run for re-election.

Already, more and more candidates declared to run against him. How would the court case play out? Would it be decisive or, like those of Trump, be superseded, delayed, or even dropped? By Trump? Inner City Press is covering all these cases in SDNY, and corruption in the UN including Turkey's Mission before that. This is the story, City of Maybe, Part I.

II. Electorate as Jury

He came into the courthouse
With his usual guards
And spoke out in the garden
Of being arrested selling counterfeits
Like on Canal Street just north

Three years later he returned indicted
For bribes from Turkey
To expedite its UN Mission

They said, Everyone does it
And it's true, the UN is full of corruption
And counterfeits are still sold on Canal

But what about the straw donations?
What about Winnie Greco
And her fakes arches
In Kim Lau Square
And before in Sunset Park?

As with the Orange Man
Maybe only an election will decide it
The electorate as jury.

III. Eric Adams on the Silk Road

Benjamin Netanyahu was fighting Palestinian statehood and Turkey's Recep Tayyip Erdogan was bruising for a fight. It was not 2024 but 2011. A security guard ended up with a broken rib - which the UN apologized to Erdogan for - and a blogger had an exclusive that would lead, along with others, to being banned from entering the UN. He would gravitate down to the SDNY courthouse where another of Erdogan's interlocutors would be indicted. Not the corruption official of the UN, which uses and abuses legal immunity, but Eric Adams.

From 2011:

Dust-Up of UN Security With Turkish Delegation Leads to Hospitalization

By Matthew Russell Lee, Exclusive

UNITED NATIONS, September 23, updated -- While Mahmoud Abbas and Benyamin

Netanyahu traded speeches about Palestinian statehood on Friday, a diplomatic incident occurred on the fourth floor of the General Assembly Hall. Sources tell Inner City Press that the Turkish delegation literally had a run-in with security in the UN, in which the Turkish prime minister Erdogan was touched.

Then, a male security official was injured and taken to the hospital, another officer also assaulted and injured. Several sources spoke of a door broken in the UN earlier in the week, attributing it to Turkey. Inner City Press observed Secretary General Ban Ki-moon's chief of staff Vijay Nambiar break in to a rare run, accompanied by UN Safety and Security chief Gregory Starr, out of the North Lawn building and on to First Avenue in the rain, crossing toward Turkey's Mission to the UN.

Later a senior UN official told Inner City Press bitterly that "Turkey is throwing its weight around," linking the incident to Turkey's anger, including at the UN, about the Palmer (and Uribe) report about the Gaza flotilla incident in which eight Turkish citizens were killed. Greg Starr and Ban Ki-moon, Nambiar and dust-up not shown The source asked, "A new muscular foreign policy -- even inside the UN building?"

Update: Inner City Press, having Friday afternoon published far and away the first story about the incident, was threatened.

And so it would be. Inner City Press' covered was picked up by The Atlantic:

Turkish Melee: The U.N. Brawl You May Have Missed

On Friday, several unnamed sources told the Inner City Press--a U.N. news site recently profiled in The New Yorker--that Erdogan had been "touched" and several people had been injured in a fight between the Turkish delegation and U.N. security guards.

Over the next 24 hours, numerous Turkish news sites (including Sabah, above) picked up the story, stressing that Ban had offered a personal apology to Erdogan for the incident. 'I'm afraid there was an unfortunate incident,' Sabah quoted Erdogan as saying"…

Erdogan's comments 13 years later on the indictment that his government bribed Eric Adams would be less diplomatic, as we shall see below.

But first, there was a harbinger indictment in state court, by DA Alvin Bragg, and Inner City Press was there, July 7, 2023:

NYS arraignments for illegal campaign contributions to Eric Adams campaign for Mayor: DWAYNE MONTGOMERY, 64, SHAMSUDDIN RIZA, MILLICENT REDICK, RONALD PEEK, YAHYA MUSHTAQ, 28, SHAHID MUSHTAQ & ECOSAFETY CONSULTANTS (video by #InnerCityPressDowntownNewsService -

Courthouse contrasts:

The mood in 40 Foley Square is dark. There are no windows in the elevator lobbies. The courtrooms are dark wood. It seems solemn, and ominous.

500 Pearl by contrast is airy and light. Yes, people are sentenced to life imprisonment - but it is all chipper and upbeat. 100 Centre Street is pure chaos.

Eric Adams Turkish UN Blues
by Matthew Russell Lee, Inner City Press

Everything for sale, in Eric Adams' city
Turkish House unsafe, but outside looking pretty
Guterres cuts the ribbon, money disappearing
Behind the COVID masks, dictators are leering

In Verizon's building, yes Phil Banks is hiding
NYPD promotions, for a little tiding

Seizing all the phones, search warrant eruption
There seems to be no end, to NYC corruption

IV. Fire Department First

The first Federal indictments were not of Adams himself, but two of his FDNY officials, in mid-September 2024. Inner City Press reported:

Amid the scandals swirling around NYC Mayor Eric Adams and his inner circle, on September 16 SDNY US Attorney Damian Williams announced two indictments, limited to the FDNY.

"Anthony Saccavino and Brian Cordasco, two former chiefs of the New York City Fire Department Bureau of Fire Prevention, are charged with bribery, corruption, and false statements offenses… in connection with a scheme to solicit and accept tens of thousands of dollars in bribe payments in exchange for providing preferential treatment to certain individuals and companies with matters pending before the BFP."

At a press conference in 26 Federal Plaza, Williams declined to comment on requests to City Hall; he said Henry Santiago Jr. is cooperating in this investigation.

Inner City Press live tweeted the arraignment, including:

Assistant US Attorney Matthew J. King: There are 3 terabytes of discovery, iCloud accounts. We'd like 2 months to produce discovery, conference in 90 days.

Judge Lewis J. Liman: I'll set a trial date at that time - December 17 at 11 am.

Cordasco's lawyer Frank Rothman: Sounds reasonable. Based on the amount of discovery, three terabytes at a minimum, I think we will need every one of those 60 days.

Saccavino's lawyer Shannon Stewart: Works for me as well, same as Mr. Rothman stated.

[Judge Liman would in October 2024 admonish previous NYC Mayor Rudy Giuliani to not try to speak for himself in court, given his Staten Island lawyer; afterward in front of the courthouse, Giuliani would say all SDNY does now is "prosecute Republicans and people like Eric Adams" after he criticized Joe Biden's and Kamala Harris' policy on immigration. Would it lead to charges against Adams going away, after Trump won the November 5, 2024 election and SDNY US Attorney Damian Williams announced he would quit on December 13? Williams held a final Q&A with media that Inner City Press attended, but it was deemed off-the-record...]

So, back to the public record, what *about* Adams and the Turkish support, expedition for the Turkish Mission to the UN?

That boot would drop next, with the indictment filed under seal on September 24, and unsealed on September 26.

V. Presentment before Magistrate Judge Parker

September 27, 2024 - Inner City Press thread:

OK - now US v Eric Adams arraignment - Adams and his lawyer Alex Spiro have been sitting waiting at defense table.

In the first row of the courtroom gallery behind Eric Adams are six of his security detail. Four prosecutors at the front table. Waiting for the judge. Drum roll...

All rise!
Alex Spiro on behalf of Mayor Adams.

Magistrate Judge Katharine H. Parker: Good afternoon, Mayor Adams. Certain charges have been issued against you. The purpose of today is to inform you of certain of your rights...

AUSA Celia V. Cohen: The defendant arrived at court at 8:45 am.

Judge Parker: I am required to release you on bond unless I find there are no conditions that could ensure your return to court, and that you are not a danger to the community. You hired your own lawyer

Judge Parker: Count 1 accuses of you wire fraud, soliciting and accepting a campaign contribution from a foreign national and Federal program bribery. You are alleged to have engaged in a number of overt acts including accept free plane tickets or upgrades

Judge Parker: ...and causing the FDNY to allow the occupation of Turkish House when it would have failed inspection. Court 2 alleges your of fraudulent matching funds, for funds that did not qualify. Also, soliciting a campaign contribution from a foreign national

Judge Parker: The indictment identifies Turkish House, 821 UN Plaza. Do you waive

a public reading of the indictment?
Adams: I waive.

Judge: How do you I plead?
Adam: I am not guilty your Honor.
Judge: Mayor Adams has pleaded not guilty.

Judge: I will enter a written order confirming the Government's Brady obligations after this proceeding. Bail or release?
AUSA: We have a proposed package, on consent. Release on the condition he not contact witnesses or individuals named in the indictment

AUSA: We will confer on a reasonable accommodation for family and staff.
Judge: What does that mean? Why not enter the condition now?
AUSA: We have not discussed which staff members
Judge: It is typical for a defendant to surrender passport

AUSA: We are not requesting he surrender his passport.
Judge: Mr. Spiro?
Spiro: There is only one name in the indictment. So they will have to tell us the names.
AUSA: We will, but not in the bond.
Judge: OK, I accept the recommendation for release

Judge: I believe that Judge Ho has set a next date?
AUSA: Wednesday October 2 at 10:30 am.
Judge: Any other matters?
AUSA: We move to exclude time under the Speedy Trial Act
Judge: Mr. Spiro?
Spiro: I don't object - but we want a speedy trial.

Adams' lawyer Spiro: We will be filing a motion to dismiss on Wednesday.
Judge: Mayor Adams, if you fail to appear in court or violate any conditions of your release, a warrant will be issued for your

arrest - not more than 10 years if the offense is a felony

Judge: I'm going to ask the Marshals to escort the Mayor to the Clerk's office... Adjourned.

VI. Eric Adams in The Bronx

My place is strength
Ain't in the night clubs
Nor even vegan pop-ups-

It's in these churches
Like this one in The Bronx
The perfect backdrop
The perfect extras to cheer
My new line: I won't resign
I will reign...

Eric Adams, The Beginning

We stole some checks
Me and my brother
And got arrested cashing them
Tuned up in the precinct
Until a brother cop said stop

I wanted be one of them
To say when to stop
And when to start

Now they're trying
To stop me…

Curtis Sliwa vs Eric

Sure I made up crimes
Early in my red-hatted career
But that I grew up
I live with cats
Eric lives in New Jersey
Blaming his taxes on a homeless man
And calling ME a clown

He's the one going to jail
I only regret
I'm not the one who arrested him…

* * *

Downtown they put up charts
My flights to Turkey and Sri Lanka
St Regis and some resort I don't remember
Resorts World - glad I didn't see that one

So here under the white tent
A guy yells, It ain't a Black thing

I have my people with me
Damn but we got / Things done for this town.

Same lawyer as Elon Musk
And he can't even get a delay
From this Ho or Hou
Who the hell is he
I'll show 'em who I am
Again they will see and know
Hou I am...

VII.   October 2, 2024 Before Judge Ho

OK - now at US v. Eric Adams on Türkiye UN Mission bribery charges, after motion to dismiss Count V and for a hearing on SDNY leaks.

Now here in Courtroom 110, Eric Adams is at the defense table, staring straight ahead, hands on his lap, Alex Spiro to his right. Four prosecutors at their table. Drum roll...

All rise! In the matter of US v Eric Adams... Alex Spiro on behalf of Mayor Adams.
Judge Ho: Good morning Mayor Adams. I want to give a road map. We'll go over some preliminary matters, we'll go over the motions that have been filed. We'll address discovery

Judge Ho: We'll discuss a trial date.
Assistant US Attorney: This case involves the defendant using his position illegally... Some

parts are per se illegal, some are illegal in context. There is wire fraud, false certifications and improper matching funds.

Judge Ho: Does the US anticipate a superseding indictment?
AUSA: Likely additional defendants, possible in separate cases.
Judge Ho: Timing on that?
AUSA: We'll analyze quickly, but I can't say.
Judge Ho: Understood

AUSA: The Speedy Trial Act clock has been tolled by the motions.
Judge Ho: Mr. Spiro, is that your understanding?
Spiro: It is not. May I use the podium?
Judge Ho: I was just asking about the Speedy Trial clock.

Spiro: They don't get a pause when they engage in misconduct-
Judge Ho: Do you have any authority for that?
Spiro: It's our position.

Judge Ho: But do you have any precedent?
Spiro: Give me a moment....

[Time passes]
Judge Ho: We can come back to the Speedy Trial clock. Do you anticipate filing any additional motions? I'd like to do it all at once.
Spiro: We do not intend to file additional motions at this time.

Judge Ho: So, typically the US has two weeks.
AUSA Hagan Scotten: We'd like four weeks. The motion alleging improper disclosure of grand jury material was surprising to us. The Mayor previously said he understand we were not, it was against our interest

AUSA Scotten: They says only the prosecution knew about the subpoenas. But they did too. We want to make a careful submission.

Judge Ho: Mr. Spiro?
Spiro: They bought this case, they decided

when to bring it, they knew we would file these motions. Their case against Mr. Benjamin was dismissed... There is a primary election on the horizon. So, two weeks.

Spiro: We could get our reply in faster than a week. There is no reason for this case to drag. I assume the government is preserving their records about the sanctions motion?

Judge Ho: Let's have the US oppositions due on October 18, a little more than two weeks

Spiro: We'll reply by October 25, under the rules.

Judge Ho: A hearing date, if we need one - on Oct 31. That's a hearing on the motions that have actually been filed.

Spiro: I have served on them a specific Brady demand about their key witness in this case

Judge Ho: Mr. Scotten, let's turn to the nature and volume of discovery.

AUSA Scotten: It's extensive. The investigation began in the summer of 2021, before the defendant had even become mail.

There's stuff from Signal applications, with the Turkish Official

AUSA Scotten: A lot of the communications, setting things up, are in Turkish. The defense may have a different view of what's important. We can translate all of it. There are bank records and a lot of records from the Turkish airline, $50,000 of flights in 2017

AUSA Scotten: We'll show that the defendant purported to be flying coach but arranged in advance for the upgrade, not on the day-of. Forms to the CFB, certifications... Ethics trainings that the defendant took as a City officials

AUSA Scotten: There are voice memos, often in Turkish. Witnesses, we expect many of them, who directly participated. Events the defendant was involved in - witnesses who made illegal contributions, then they got a message from the defendant. I can't get into more

AUSA Scotten: There has been witness intimidation. The defendant today gave us a hard drive, we can load it up with discovery once Your Honor signs the protective order. We'll give them electronic records, the NYC DOI investigation...

AUSA Scotten: One year ago today Senator Menendez had his initial conference - and Judge Stein said, discovery by December

AUSA Scotten: The defendant's cell phone, he changed the passport --
Adams's lawyer Spiro: I object to this ten minute presentation. I get that it's a tell, that their case is weak.
Judge Ho: I don't find that Mr. Scotten has done anything inappropriate. Continue

Judge Ho: Can you clone the phone if you can't unlock it?
AUSA Scotten: No. Additionally, the City may hold a privilege over certain of his communications. More recently seized

devices will take longer. We can't give him everything. We have to follow the warrant

AUSA Scotten: There are several related investigations too, we will tell them about them.

Judge Ho: You mentioned that is will be searchable by the defendant?

AUSA Scotten: Text searchable. They can put it in a database.

Judge Ho: So December, like Menendez?

AUSA Scotten: Dec 15?

Judge Ho: In the Menendez case it was earlier December, if memory serves. December 4. [He's been reading the Menendez docket, it seems]

Spiro: They claim they're comply by December 4. We'll see. They are digging into immigrant communities

Eric Adams' lawyer Spiro: I'm not sure why they think all contacts with immigrant communities are suspicious. If they provide us the information with all due speed, fine.

Judge Ho: Discovery by December 4, on a

rolling basis.
Spiro: Their key witness is lying

Adams' lawyer Spiro: All four of them know that their key witnesses has said different things. But they have not given it to me.
Judge Ho: If it's produced by Dec 4, how much time do you need, Mr. Spiro?
Spiro: If any part of this case survives our motions, speedy

Judge Ho: How much time?
Adams' lawyer Spiro: 2 weeks. December 18.
AUSA Scotten: We'd like ours not due January 1... How about January 6?
Spiro: Fine. We'll reply in a week, Jan 13.
Judge Ho: A control date for a hearing on January 27

Judge Ho: If discovery is due on December 4, let's have an interim conference on December 5 - any conflicts?
Adams' lawyer Spiro: That date may be tricky. Anyway we'd want the next week.
Judge Ho: OK... December 13

AUSA Scotten: We anticipate litigation under the Classified Information Procedures Act, CIPA

[Inner City Press recently got CIPA transcripts unsealed, by SDNY District Judge Jesse M. Furman, in the CIA Wikileaks case of US v. Joshua Schulte, reportedly "making CIPA history." Would there be more public CIPA precedents to win in US v. Eric Adams, if the prosecution continues to move forward?]

Eric Adams' lawyer Spiro: They are trying to delay the trial. We will not object to the CIPA materials - if there are *ex parte* communication, or this suggestions under this rubric. I am not interested in challenging it. The defense effectively does not care

AUSA Scotten: With all due respect I'm not sure my adversary understands CIPA. I'm not sure he can waive court review.

Judge Ho: You've flagged it. Let's talk trial. How long with the US case take?

AUSA Scotten: We would propose four weeks, for the entire trial.

Adams' lawyer Spiro: We think all they have is a week, admissible evidence. Us, two days... We are asking for a trial date. They indicted the sitting Mayor of New York, there is a primary. We are not waiving the Speedy Trial Act for even one day. Conclude in March

Eric Adams' lawyer Spiro: There are primary ballots to be printed. That's in March. So we want the case done before that.

Judge Ho: I was looking up at the ceiling because I was trying to figure out election timing. Interest is heightened but what are the dates?

Adams' lawyer Spiro: Next year it is the first week of April... To be on the ballot you have to go through a process, even the incumbent. We have a right under the Sixth Amendment.

Judge Ho: Why before the certification? June 24, with early voting before.

Adams' lawyer Spiro: Of all the politicians in New York, they picked this guy. So let's have this trial in March. I can't imagine that the US would object.

Judge Ho: When are signatures collected?
Spiro: February.
Judge Ho: So you want February?
Spiro: March

AUSA Scotten: It's in the court's discretion. Setting the trial date today won't expedite anything. I don't think defendant wants to waive his appellate rights
Adams' lawyer Spiro: The People of the State of New York want this date, March. I will be ready in March

Adams' lawyer Spiro: This case was brought a month before the national election. We will not waive Speedy Trial Act.
Judge Ho: The Menendez case got to trial in May. I'll take it under advisement for today,

I'll set the trial date soon. I want to consider it

Judge Ho: Last week we had some requests about the timing of the arraignment. The defense asked for Dec 27 or Dec 30. I set it for Dec 27, which caused a lot of work. I got two emails to Chambers, due to logistical problems that were unspecified

Judge Ho: There's a presumption of public access to judicial documents.
[Note: Inner City Press has filed with Judge Ho in another case, about DOJ seeking to seize a Russian oligarch's yacht - so far, not entirely transparent]

Judge Ho: I've found Mayor Adams has been represented by Wilmer Hale. One of my NAACP colleagues is now a partner there. I am disclosing in an abundance of caution. Also, in 2018 I served on the NYC Charter Revision Commission, it did not alter who can contribute

Judge Ho: If either side wants to file a motion to recuse me, do so by October 18. Now, the Speedy Trial clock. First, times for the hearings we've put on the calendar. Oct 31 - let's hold that on Nov 1, at 2 pm. Dec 13 at 2 pm

Judge Ho: On Speedy Trial, any US motion? AUSA Scotten: It seems the court is already excluding time to December 13. The Moreno case they cite is about an entirely different section. We move to exclude until Dec 13. Judge Ho: I can also exclude as a complex case

Adams' lawyer Spiro: The Moreno case is about prosecutorial misconduct, delay in finding a witness. This is not a complex case. One allegation of bribery, and $10,000 of donor funds matched. There are not lots of defendants. The public has a strong interest

Adams' lawyer Spiro: We want this case to be done in March. We would be ready in February. The Gambino case says, Set the trial date early. My practice involves reporting to other judges all over the country

Judge Ho: Thank you Mr. Spiro. Time is excluded

Judge Ho: Speedy Trial Act time is excluded. We are adjourned.

VIII. FDNY Plea, Presentment of Bahi

Next would come a guilty plea in the first FDNY case - and the arrest of Adams staffer Mohamed Bahi, with the possibility that he would flip (and become a cooperator, like others) already in the air.

Inner City Press' Cordasco guilty plea thread:

OK - now at FDNY guilty plea of Brian Cordasco

All rise!

Judge: Is there an application?

Defense: Mr. Cordasco wants to plead guilty.
Judge: Let me ask you about yourself.

Cordasco: 50, BA from Fairfield University --
Judge: Where is that?

Cordasco: Connecticut.

Judge: The maximum penalty is 5 years in prison.

Judge: There is, however, a written plea agreement. It has a stipulated sentencing guideline range of 87 to 108 month - but it's capped at 60 months.

Judge: Tell me what you did.

Cordasco: Between 2021 and 2023 I received more than $5000 to expedite in FDNY.
AUSA: He conspired with Mr. Saccavino and Henry Santiago Jr

Judge: I accept the guilty plea. Sentencing January 14

P.S. - due to defense counsel medical issue, sentencing moved back to February 19, 2025, which Judge calls a hard date, not to be changed.

Inner City Press will cover that -and today, newly arrested Eric Adams (ex) staffer Mohamed Bahi too:

OK - now at presentment of Eric Adams' ex-staffer Mohamed Bahi, charged with deleting his Signal messages with Adams about straw donations as the FBI seized his phone. Inner City Press is on the cases and will live tweet, thread below

[This week's Magistrate Judge in SDNY is Robert W. Lehrburger - yesterday Inner City Press reported his arraignment of a defendant for having gun parts from China...

[Bahi is brought out by US Marshals in an Under Armor shirt, is whispering with his lawyer.]

All rise!
Deputy: Presentment of Mohamed Bahi, 24 Magistrate 3535.
Defense: I am only on this for the presentment

Judge: Time of arrest?
AUSA: Today at 6:20 am.

Judge: Mr. Bahi, you are charged with obstruction of justice and destruction of records in connection with alleged straw donations to a candidate for, uh, Mayor

Judge: You do have retained counsel for today. Have you reviewed the complaint?
Counsel: Yes.
Judge: Because this is a complaint you have the right to a preliminary hearing.... We'll set a date in a bit. But now we are going to address if you can be released.

AUSA: We propose release on $250,000 bond co-signed by two financially responsible person, and the Pre-Trial conditions with the exception of Condition 5

AUSA: No contact with co-conspirators or witnesses in this case outside of the presence of his counsel.
Judge: Acceptable to the defense?
Counsel: They are, Your Honor.

Judge: These terms are acceptable to the Court. Mr. Bahi, you will be released on those terms. If you fail to adhere - fail to appear or violate the conditions - a warrant will be issued for your arrest, the bond must be bail, you can be charged with bail jumping

Judge: We are adjourned.

IX. Circle (Firing Squad) of Commissioners

Mohamed Bahi

In Adams' world
It was popular
To liaise with the Turks
And take their straw donations

When the Feds came down
To take my phone
Yeah, Signal came off
Now they call it obstruction
If Eric thinks
I'll do five years for him
As if he were Assad
Or Erdogan
He's crazy

Ingrid

It's so clean in Japan
And so dirty back here in New York
They take your phones at JFK

And threaten to arrest you
I was gonna resign
But now I'll stand by my brother
Eric, I'll go down with his ship

Phil Banks

I wasn't always hiding here
In my white Verizon building
Rechnitz took me to Israel
To shoot an automatic weapon
And to Vegas with the hookers

Eric and me we get shit done
Now these prissy wokester
Not even brown most of 'em
Say he should resign
For what he said he about the hustle
And that hotel on 45th Street
We can't even make money off...
The Irish did it.
The Italians did it.
It's our time
Until it isn't.

Eric Adams, Purple Potatoes

So what my son
Live in the Windham Garden
So what the Stop Work order
Went away from Mrs. Hu?

It wasn't the straw donations
Winnie being Winnie
It was those purple potatoes
Vegan God of outer boroughs…

Tabloid Photog

They tell me an Asian woman
Is about to be indicted
And to wait out here on Worth Street
Instead of outside Penny

Then they tell me, Never mind
Delete all the photos
So we don't get sued.
Whatever.

Eric and Jessica

One Police Commissioner quit
After the Feds seized his phones
I put in a hard-ass Irishman
And they raided him too, right away
So what? A billionaire's daughter
Let's see them go after her

Eric Adams Sheena Wright Mets Blues
by Matthew Russell Lee, Inner City Press,
Oct 5, 2024

Sheena Wright in sweats, saying that it's all private
Keechant to the Mets, Tim's acting like a pirate
Hakeem says to stay, Cuomo doing polling
Indictments one week pause but the head keep rolling

Most are talking Turkey but what of Winnie Greco?
Not so long ago, they were all drinking prosecco
Eric and his Spyro say they want it speedy
Fast and loose' one thing but who could be so greedy?

Eric Adams Uzbek Straw Donations Blues
by Matthew Russell Lee, Inner City Press,
Oct 12, 2024

Four Uzbek businessmen
Send Mohamed Bahi to meet with them
Ten thousand dollars, break it in five
When the Fed show up, respond with lies

Every week, a new indictment
To Tish and Andy it's just incitement
Each of them wants to rule Room 9
Kathy dropping the axe, just a matter of time

Eric Adams Legal Defense Fund Blues
by Matthew Russell Lee, Inner City Press,
Oct 19, 2024

Winnie Greco and China, it all falls away
At every agency, City of pay to play
Move to dismiss at least Count Five
Go on the podcast but not always live

Legal defense fund is running low
When it hits zero the lawyers will go

Mohamed Bahi - who pays his fee?
Oh for the times propping up OTB

Eric Adams Matching Fund Blues
by Matthew Russell Lee, Inner City Press,
Oct 26, 2024

Matching fund, who needs 'em?
Cease and desist, who heeds 'em?
Grand jury notes, got Rana
No love… from Ro Khanna

Eric Adams

Raise the flag, of the Grenadines
Living in Jersey, eating clementines
Roll up in black cars, show him the money
To Eric Adams, everything still funny

Eric Adams 40 Foley Andrew Cuomo Blues
by Matthew Russell Lee, Inner City Press,
Nov 2, 2024

Big day / in Forty Foley
Ruben Diaz / getting holy
Turkish upgrade / Nickle and diming
Big Fight / on election timing

Eric Adams

Forget Cuomo / Watch Mamdani
Killed by Freeman / Not Ohtani
Not Spiro / But Bash
Tokyo trips / Turkish cash?

X. Interlude, Bling Bishop Lamor Whitehead

It was December 2022, after Eric Adams speech in the SDNY garden but nearly two years before his indictment, when a pastor or bishop linked to him was indicted, initially for promising access to and favors from Adams - a charge the prosecutors later walked away from.

Inner City Press covered US v. Lamor Whitehead from presentment to conviction and beyond.

Presentment December 19, 2022:

OK- now in SDNY Mag Court for US v Lamor Whitehead for fraud, after covering him as robbery victim in EDNY

Whitehead is in a white hooded sweatshirt, with a retained lawyer. AUSA says he was arrested today at 6 am.

Magistrate Judge Gabriel W. Gorenstein describes wire fraud and threat of force to obtain money from a Bronx business; also lie about not having a 2d cell phone. US agrees to $500,000 unsecured bond, a week for 2 signatures. Jersey travel allowed.

Assistant US Attorney: He is to be released today on his own signature. Defense: He has never had a passport.

Jump cut to the trial, February 26, 2024

OK - now in US v. Lamor Whitehead (Bling Bishop throwing around name of Eric Adams), seating the jury then opening arguments

Courtroom deputy: Do each of you swear to follow the evidence so help you God? [Yes] Please be seated.
[Non-selected jurors leave]
Judge Schofield: These notebooks, you can put your name on the inside. No one else can see them. They're just an aid

Judge Schofield: Direct evidence is testimony by a witness about that they saw, or heard, or did. You may consider circumstantial evidence. The opening statements are not evidence. The lawyers will tell you what they expect the evidence will show

Judge Schofield: You may hear testimony of law enforcement officials, or of clergymen. They are not worthy of more consideration than an ordinary witness. Everyone has prejudices that we may or may not be aware of... There is implicit bias, it can impact us

Judge Schofield: This is a criminal case. All parties stand equal here. The defendant is charged with wire fraud, attempted wire fraud and extortion, false statements- the defendant has pleaded guilty (!) [Sidebar]
Judge: He has pleaded NOT guilty, I made an error

Judge Schofield: You'll be asked to return a verdict on each count. Counts 1 and 5 are for wire fraud. Count 1 is about Ms. Anderson and her son, both of whom attended the defendant's church. Count 5 is about June 2018, a loan application.

Judge Schofield: It is now 3:54, we're going take a short bathroom break then have opening statements.
[Opening arguments will be here - watch this feed

All rise, jury entering!
Judge Schofield: Government?
Assistant US Attorney: This is a case about fraud. About a con man who made false promises, threats and intimidation. That con man is Lamor Whitehead.

AUSA: He was the bishop - he was a friend of the Mayor of NYC. He abused that trust by lying again & again. He lied about how much money he had. All with the goal of getting money to fund his extravagant lifestyle. He wore designer clothes - nothing wrong with it

AUSA: He is charged with defrauding a church goer, a money transmitter, and a

Bronx businessman. The defendant's first scheme targeted a single mother whose adult son was a church member. He conned her out of $90,000 for a fixer-upper home

AUSA: The defendant spent it on Louis Vuitton, GrubHub, on and on. In the 2d scheme, he conned a lender on a $250,000 loan... Then there was the shop owner who fixed his Mercedes. The owner refused to pay. The defendant lied about real estate. He said for $500,000

AUSA: He claimed he could get the Mayor to do favors. The Mayor was a friend and mentor, yes. But he had never gotten favors from the Mayor. Finally, he lied to the FBI. In 2022 they had a search warrant for cell phones. They got one; he said he had no more. Lie

AUSA: You'll hear from the lender, you'll then hear from the Bronx body shop owner. The defendant claimed the Mayor will do whatever I want - and that he had guns in his church, "I will hurt you." And the lies to the FBI. For now we ask you to pay attention

AUSA: Use your common sense - you will reach the only conclusion that the defendant is guilty.

Judge Schofield: Defense?

Dawn Florio, for Whitehead: I want to thank each and every one of you. The government had to prove all that, and extinguish reasonable doubt

Dawn Florio: You're going to hear a lot of testimony - pay attention. Are they credible? Look at the lack of evidence. Rasheed got the money from his mother by promising her he would buy her a house. He bought his own house, with his mother's signature

Dawn Florio: You will hear that Pauline complained her son used her credit to get his own home - it was Rasheed who lied to his mother. I do not expect there to be any credible evidence Lamor Whitehead told Pauline he would get her a house. Why would he?

Dawn Florio: Count 1 belongs in civil court, not Federal court

AUSA: Objection

Judge Schofield: Overruled

Dawn Florio: In the civil case they allege he used the $90,000 on a 2d home for himself. Here, they're talking luxury goods. Count 2 is about Brandon Belmonte

Dawn Florio: Lamor Whitehead did not promise any specific government action on the stop work order. Lamor Whitehead kept the specifics close to his chest because that was what he was getting paid for. Count 3? Belmonte fixed Lamor's wife's car

Dawn Florio: Many can relate to this, when you take your car to the oil shop, it takes forever and forever. It wasn't nice that Lamor Whitehead said, but it was not a crime. Count 2 says he wanted $500,000 - so why extort $5000? It doesn't make sense.

Dawn Florio: Did he mislead the FBI agents? Listen carefully to what they asked him. He asked if he had another phone he could be reached on - I'm sure many of you have a work and private phone. So it wasn't false.

Dawn Florio: How can Lamor Whitehead be said to have committed fraud when he was declining loans? 1 thing that has been constant- what has the government actually proven? Their case has holes in it. A trial is like buying a house. You have to consider many factors

Dawn Florio: The direct examination is like the exterior of the house. The cross examination in the interior. You must consider both. You must consider bias and jealousy. Lamor Whitehead is not required to testify. He is fighting these charges like Adonis Creed

Dawn Florio: You are the triers of fact. Your mind must be open like a parachute. Find him not guilty.
Judge Schofield: First witness - we'll go to 4:55.
[many leave the courtroom]

Witness Brad Thornton of NerdWallet, previously Fundera - a loans marketplace

AUSA: What were your jobs at Fundera?
Thornton: We'd take in-bound leads, liaise with lenders.
AUSA: Are you familiar with their records?
Thornton: Yes. We had our office on William Street, near here.
AUSA: In June of 2018, where did applications go?
Thornton: HQ

AUSA: Who were the lenders Fundera worked with?
Thornton: PayPal, and a bank in Florida, and Kabbage
AUSA: How would Fundera send materials?
Thornton: We had an API integration with the lender... We could speak together.

AUSA: Who filled in this info?
Thornton: The applicant. Lamor Whitehouse. Anointing Management Service. They got pre-qualified.
AUSA: What did they claim as income?

Thornton: $312,000.

AUSA: Is the personal information here part of owner info?

Thornston: Yes

AUSA: Here is a stipulation with the defendant... This Eric Adams' phone number... This is Pauline Anderson's Bank of America account number. Let's go back to GX 407-02-1. Scroll down. What is this service authorization box?

Thornton: So we can submit the info

AUSA: What are these?

Thornton: Bank statements uploaded by the applicant.

Judge Schofield: The witness may step down, and be here at 10 am. The rest, be here at 9:45 am.

There's more after jury leaves.

Judge Schofield: The government has subpoenaed a reporter. I aim to conduct an in camera, ex parte inquiry into whether source information will be sought. The US does not

object. Defense?
Dawn Florio: No objection

Judge Schofield: I will rule either this evening in writing or first thing tomorrow morning. What's the game plan?
AUSA: 20 more minutes of Mr. Thornton - then PayPal and Wells Fargo representatives.
Judge Schofield: We are adjourned.

February 27, 2024

I US v. Lamor Whitehead, mother of congregant Rasheed is on the witness stand.

AUSA: Who did you understand Mr. Whitehead to be helping?
Pauline Anderson: I believe the team Rasheed was working with to get his house was recommended by Mr. Whitehead.
AUSA: How long did it take?
Pauline Anderson: Four months. I co-signed for the mortgage.

AUSA: What had lowered your credit score?
Pauline Anderson: I co-signed others' loans - my niece and for my son Miguel - and they were behind
AUSA: What is a downpayment?
Pauline Anderson: A sizeable sum you put down.

AUSA: Who paid the downpayment for Rasheed's home?
Pauline Anderson: He did.
AUSA: When did you first see Rasheed's home?
Pauline Anderson: Before the closing.
AUSA: Who was at the closing?
Pauline Anderson: Mr. Whitehead was there...

AUSA: Who presided over Rasheed and his wife's wedding?
Pauline Anderson: Mr. Whitehead.
AUSA: When he had surgery - did you speak with Mr. Whitehead?
Pauline Anderson: He offered prayers. I really believed he was a man of God

AUSA: Did they come a time when Mr. Whitehead got involved in your process?
Pauline Anderson: Yes. I was planning to take out $50,000 from my retirement in TransAmerica.
AUSA: Did you follow Mr. Whitehead's advice?
Pauline Anderson: Yes. I thought he was truthful

AUSA: If not for Mr. Whitehead's advice, how much would have taken out of your retirement?
Pauline Anderson: $50,000.
AUSA: Where did you make the transfer?
Pauline Anderson: To my BofA account.
AUSA: Here, how much was taken out?
Pauline Anderson: $100,000

AUSA: Are you familiar with Sean Carson?
Pauline Anderson: A loan officer. Mr. Whitehead connected me with him.
AUSA: What did Mr. Carson say?
Pauline Anderson: That I couldn't get a loan.

AUSA: What was your understanding when Mr. Whitehead would find you a house?
Pauline Anderson: 6 months.
AUSA: What did you expect to lose?
Pauline Anderson: Nothing.
AUSA: How did you make the $90,000 payment to Mr. Whitehead?
PA: Check, from BofA

AUSA: How much was this for?
Pauline Anderson: $90,015.
AUSA: What did you think Mr. Whitehead would do?
Pauline Anderson: That I would see properties. But we only went to see one property. Rasheed was there - and two more from Mr. Whitehead's church

Pauline Anderson: We saw two houses in New Jersey.
AUSA: What did you think of them?
Pauline Anderson: They were small and narrow. Next to a train station, it passed while we were there. A turn off for me.

AUSA: Did you tell Mr. Whitehead?
PA: Yes.

AUSA: How did you communicate with Mr. Whitehead?
Pauline Anderson: By phone. Never email or text.

AUSA: Did you get concerned?
PA: Yes, I told Rasheed. [voice breaks] I'd ask him, what's happening? He said Mr. Whitehead was busy with his campaign for Bklyn BP

AUSA: How many $100 payments did you get from Mr. Whitehead?
Pauline Anderson: Twice, in 2021. It was supposed to be interest. My focus was not so much on the $100, I thought the time span of getting the house would be short.

AUSA: How did you ask for money back?
Pauline Anderson: Mr. Whitehead gave Rasheed $5000 cash in an envelope
AUSA: Was your landlord showing where you lived?
PA: Yes. A couple seemed interested. I

thought, I might not have a place to go to, for my mom and sister

AUSA: What were you told about getting your money back?

Pauline Anderson: I kept hearing Mr. Whitehead was campaigning.

AUSA: Was there a disagreement between Mr. Whitehead and Rasheed?

PA: Yes. His wife had just had a traumatic delivery, at Lenox Hill Hospital

AUSA: Can you read this text you sent to Mr. Whitehead?

[Pauline Anderson does - and cries. Inner City Press aims to publish exhibits from this trial]

Pauline Anderson is still crying]

AUSA: Did you ever get a contract?

PA: No.

AUSA: You wrote, I need a return of the money -

PA: Yes.

AUSA: And he wrote that Rasheed had been

disrespectful. "I am a man of integrity, you will not lose, I just gave him $5K.

AUSA: What did you write to Mr. Whitehead?
Pauline Anderson: We need to discuss when I get the money back.
AUSA: Mr. Whitehead wrote back, suddenly there's urgency after Rasheed gets disrespectful. That he couldn't pay until August

AUSA: What here were you thinking?
Pauline Anderson: I was panicking, that I'd lose the money. That's why I was texting.
AUSA: Did Rasheed show you texts?
PA: Yes. Mr. Whitehead was berating Rasheed, asking God to exact vengeance on him

Judge Schofield: Is this a good place to end?
AUSA: Yes.
Jury leaves.
Judge Schofield: We'll resume tomorrow.

From March 11, 2024

In US v Lamor Whitehead rebuttal summation, prosecutor says he lied on the stand, that blaming Rasheed was a distraction.

AUSA: Whitehead threatened Brandon Belmonte with violence, to get money. He said, "Eric Adams will do what I want" but only if the property was transferred to him (Whitehead). Then he lied to the FBI.

AUSA: Whitehead thought you could fool you too - he is guilty as charged.

VERDICT ON BLING BISHOP: Jury Finds Lamor **Whitehead** Guilty on All Five Counts in Trial with Eric Adams Cited

May 1, 2024:

In Trial Bishop Lamor Whitehead Guilty with Eric Adams Cited -- Now US Wants [and Gets] Remand to Jail Pre-Sentencing, after an email about threats, US says discovery material misused

XI. ICE Information, Straw Donors

In June 2024, a former Director of Constituent Services in the NYC Mayor's Office Tommy Lin was indicted and arrested for bank fraud.

In November 2024 an ICE Deportation Officer Henry Yau was arrested and presented in SDNY for leaking ICE information, with NYC official Tommy Lin cited. Inner City Press was the only media present for Yau's presentment, and reported:

SDNY COURTHOUSE, Nov 21 – The US Attorney's Office for the Southern District of

New York on November 21 announced "the arrest of HENRY YAU for a scheme to commit identity theft, convert government records, and disclose agency records containing individually identifiable information. YAU will be presented before Magistrate Judge Stewart D. Aaron."

Inner City Press went to the proceeding, and as the only media there live tweeted it, from the thread:

Yau is brought in by US Marshals, in turquoise t-shirt and COVID mask. He has retained counsel.

Magistrate Judge Stewart D. Aaron: Time of arrest? AUSA: 7 am. Judge: Detention or release? AUSA: Bail package

Defense: I'd like to push this to second call Note: YAU disclosed confidential information from law enforcement databases about Victim-1 who Lin was seeking to deported from the US due to conflict with members of a bank fraud conspiracy in which Lin was involved

They're back on Yau. AUSA: We propose release on $2 million bond, $1 million [of which] in cash or property Judge: What's the hang up? [A third retained lawyer has gotten involved] Defense: This bail is excessive. Mr. Yau owns some investment properties. 3d call?

AUSA: There was an audit of his DHS downloads, he took passwords - we want to search his residence or we'll freeze it Defense: We offer $1 million signature, $250,000 secured. AUSA: He traveled around the world chasing fugitives for ICE. He knows how to flee

AUSA: They tried to run his social security number - others have been searching him, other law enforcement seemingly working with him Judge: I am the one who signs search warrants. If probable cause is shown I will keep him detained pending the search Judge: I give you 30 minutes.

They're back again on US v Henry Yau No contact with Tommy Lin without counsel present. Yau is signing something - public? Is he giving back the DHS info?

The case is US v. Yau, 24-mj-4055 (Aaron)

Later in November 2024 Inner City Press surmised:

"The complaint said Yau gave / sold the information to "a former candidate for New York City Council and New York State Assembly ('CC-1')" - Inner City Press surmises is may be Dao Yin, who ran for the Council in 2019 then against Ron Kim for Assembly. So were the ICE names to get matching funds?"

XII. November 1, 2024 before Judge Ho

OK - now at US v. Eric Adams, argument on his motion to dismiss Count V, the Turkish bribery count.

All rise!
Judge Ho: Defense?
[Speaking for Eric Adams is not Alex Spiro, seated next to him, but rather John Bash from Quinn Emanuel in Austin, Texas]
Adams' lawyer Bash: They have a pressure theory - they have not alleged enough. If this is pressure, anything is

Adams' lawyer Bash: US v. Stringer says that for some offenses, you do need to state the facts. But even if you didn't have to, when the US does state the facts, they have to be accurate. In Fischer, the Court remanded

Judge Ho: Before the Supreme Court's Snyder decision, we had to follow the decision in Ng Lap Seng [UN corruption case, UN Q&A here:

Judge Ho: Thank you, Mr. Bash. AUSA Hagen?

Assistant US Attorney Hagan Scotten: It's Scotten, Your Honor.

Judge Ho: I'm sorry.

AUSA Scotten: There are a litany of cases that support us, Snyder is obviously more recent.

AUSA Scotten: Here in SDNY Judge Rochon recent denied a Snyder motion to dismiss, in Starks [NYCHA bribery case that Inner City Press is also covering]

AUSA Scotten: The Snyder issues can be addressed at trial, in a jury instruction as Judge Kaplan did in the recent US v. Harris trial

Judge Ho: Does the indictment tell me when the quid pro quo took place?

AUSA Scotten: Prior to Sept 2021... There was also the agreement to not meet with certain people, at the request of the Turkish government. Compare it to the Silver case, about rent regulation

Judge Ho: As I understand your case, you are saying his ability to pressure was based more on having secured the Democratic line for Mayor, rather than as Brooklyn Borough President?

AUSA Scotten: His official position gets him in the room

AUSA Scotten: The Fire Commission could say, the Bronx BP, I knew where he's going to be in six months. But this guy...

Judge Ho: As a nominee, he is not an elected official.. which actions are the quo in the TCO?

AUSA Scotten: Causing FDNY to issue the letter

Judge: OK, the reply.

Adams' lawyer: The prosecutor couldn't say what the quo is. You pointed out that a mere candidate would not be liable, only if they had a prior official position. They say they'll fix it in jury instructions. That's not what they're for

Adams' lawyer Bash: The hotel lounge, it's June 2021. The permit is not until September 2021. They're vaguing this up... My friend Mr. Scotten couldn't even name the quo. On this theory, they could go to nearly any politicians house and allege this

Adams' lawyer Bash: We urge the Court to dismiss Count V.

Judge Ho: It's submitted. I'll attempt to rule shortly. Now, on the schedule. I understand Mayor Adams wanted a March 2025 trial, and the US said late May is more realistic.

AUSA Scotten: May is fine.

Judge Ho: I want a realistic date. I want to take into account the known unknowns. What about the superseding indictment you've said is likely?

AUSA Scotten: It remains unchanged. But it should not delay this trial. If it comes too late, you can sever.

Judge Ho: Mr. Spiro, your position is the same?

Spiro: Yes. I could say more-

Judge Ho: That's fine, it was yes or no. This is in open court, so we are limited what we can say about CIPA [the Classified Information Procedures Act] The US proposal is for early May

Spiro: This gets into the unknown question I could ask the court to give less weight to. We want an open, public trial in March. I'll waive CIPA is we need to. Speedy Trial is important to Mayor Adams and his defense.

Spiro: They knew this CIPA would run us up into the election. This man wants to clear his name and serve this city. If I have to give up the CIPA information, I will. We're going to let 3 letter agencies impact the most important city in the world?

Judge Ho: If the trial is completed before the start of voting, what is the prejudice?
Spiro: I don't have a degree in political science. But this is a burden
Judge Ho: Where is the cut off? The signature gather date, I don't think we can meet: February 25.

Judge Ho: Ballot certification is April 21, right?
Spiro: I don't want to quibble. You're supposed to come to court a presumed innocent man. They decided when to indict. One day we'll find out why. You saw their little press conference.

Spiro: You see the polls, everyone things he's guilty. And here we are, debating if the charge even survives.
Judge Ho: That's just one of the counts, Mr. Spiro.
Spiro: Then you're left with a straw donor case. There have been straw donors since the beginning.

Judge Ho: I've looked back at the Senator Ted Stevens trial, they put their foot on the gas but it raised issues.

Adams' lawyer Spiro: That trial was seven weeks. This is a relatively simple case, in my judgment

Judge Ho: The Brian Benjamin case never got to trial, but it would have been nine months. Menendez, the most recent, that one I'm looking at

Judge Ho: We can shoot for a faster trial - I'm going to set a trial date of April 21, 2025. I'm not going to set a CIPA schedule right now

Judge Ho: We'll adjourn the December 13 conference to December 20.

XIII. Eric Adams and Election(s)

Eric Adams New US Attorney Blues
by Matthew Russell Lee, Inner City Press,
Nov 9, 2024

Vote early / Say not for Orange Man
Center right / that's the man's plan
Skip Somos / Let them chatter
Bank account / Getting fatter

Eric Adams

Mohammed Bahi / Might plead out
Campaign coffers / fast bleed out
New Garland / Could dismiss it
Escalade ruling / Eric would miss it

* * *

Ghost of Eric Adams
Seen in the rotunda
Tim Pearson going in
A sealed case in the Mag Court
Conspiracy of ghosts

Eric Adams New US Attorney Blues
by Matthew Russell Lee, Inner City Press,
Nov 16, 2024

Hold on / For Jay Clayton
Down at Somos / Call Eric Satan
Kathy Hochel / Spin congestion
Switch parties / One suggestion

Eric Adams

Turk bizman / CIA asset
Fundraiser / out in Manhasset
Straw donors / five course dinner
Next Fall / Could be a winner

Eric Adams After Election Day

I'm trying to show I got this
After Trump elected
But all they want to ask me
Is how it changes my case.
I walk out.

Eric Adams New Commissioners Blues
by Matthew Russell Lee, Inner City Press,
Nov 23, 2024

One week / four slashings
Eric's rivals / are clashing
Mohamed Bahi / sitting pretty
Nixon echo / G. Gordon Liddy

Eric Adams

Cut a deal / City of Yes
Outer boroughs / Pastors bless
April Fools Day / Move the trial
Damian out / Eric's smile

The above is US v. Eric Adams, Part I - Part II and onward coming, by Inner City Press

www.ingramcontent.com/pod-product-compliance
Lightning Source LLC
Chambersburg PA
CBHW071653240526
45469CB00023B/2367